A LAKOTA WARRIOR'S HEART

A book of poetry about culture, life and love

Lawrence John Janis

Edited by:
Elizabeth A. Garcia-Janis

BALBOA.PRESS
A DIVISION OF HAY HOUSE

Balboa Press books may be ordered through booksellers or by contacting:

Balboa Press
A Division of Hay House
1663 Liberty Drive
Bloomington, IN 47403
www.balboapress.com
844-682-1282

Because of the dynamic nature of the Internet, any web addresses or
links contained in this book may have changed since publication and
may no longer be valid. The views expressed in this work are solely those
of the author and do not necessarily reflect the views of the publisher,
and the publisher hereby disclaims any responsibility for them.

The author of this book does not dispense medical advice or prescribe the
use of any technique as a form of treatment for physical, emotional, or medical
problems without the advice of a physician, either directly or indirectly. The
intent of the author is only to offer information of a general nature to help you
in your quest for emotional and spiritual well-being. In the event you use any
of the information in this book for yourself, which is your constitutional right,
the author and the publisher assume no responsibility for your actions.

Any people depicted in stock imagery provided by Getty Images are
models, and such images are being used for illustrative purposes only.
Certain stock imagery © Getty Images.

Print information available on the last page.

ISBN: 978-1-9822-6259-4 (sc)
ISBN: 978-1-9822-6261-7 (hc)
ISBN: 978-1-9822-6260-0 (e)

Library of Congress Control Number: 2021901312

Balboa Press rev. date: 01/27/2021

Introduction

A Lakota Warrior's Heart is a compilation of poems written by an amazingly extraordinary poet who simply writes straight from his heart. Our poet, Lawrence John Janis, has captured the essence of the soul of his community and his tribe through his profound poetry. His poems about the struggles and sufferings, as well as the resilience of his people, allow the reader to empathize with what the Lakotas have gone through and still go through even at present.

His many years of service in his community as a drug and alcohol counselor specialist and his work with Human Services add to the depth of his life experiences. He opened his heart to us all through his rhythmic words, to help others understand what it means to be a Lakota in the past and present world.

Lawrence authentically shared many aspects of his life through his poems and that included his own trials and tribulations. His raw and honest writings about his own life journey, addressing the shadows and lights of his soul, impels the reader to relate with both his pain and joy regarding his circumstances. Some of his poems can be piercing to the heart, some imbue the necessary jolt to create awareness and some will melt the readers' hearts as they had mine.

Having been a sun dancer for 30 years, a pipe carrier and a man who loves his Creator and his family most of all, he is able to share glimpses of his spiritual journey through this beautiful art of poetry.

In some of his poems, he tackled the challenging issues of elder abuse, child abuse, drug and alcoholism that have plagued the reservation. Through his words, he created heartfelt awareness of these issues that people generally may want to deny.

Many of his poems were featured on KILI radio and he was granted national awards for his brilliant poetry. He also addressed his people's pain from historical trauma in his poems.

Lawrence is a soulful and prayerful warrior with a heart who loves deeply and unabashedly. I feel blessed and fortunate to be a recipient of his love and cherish some of his poetry regarding the love God gifted both of us.

May you read his moving poems with a loving mind so you can allow yourselves to be in touch with your own profound sense of compassion and love. May your hearts be open to share your own ability to be truthful and real, much like A Lakota Warrior's Heart.

Elizabeth A Garcia-Janis
author
The Phoenix Miracle
The Courage to Encourage
Your Compassionate Nature

Dedication

This poetry book is lovingly dedicated to my mom and dad,
my siblings and my adult children -
Tuki, Miko and Lawrence
and my beloved grandchildren.

This book is also dedicated to family and
friends who have encouraged me through
the years with experiences and words.

Also to Elizabeth A. Garcia-Janis - as this book will
not be possible if not for her. A heartfelt thank you.

Acknowledgments

My gratitude goes to my high school Literature teacher Mr. Koss, who encouraged me with a little pin that he gave me as a compliment to my writing. That gave me confidence to continue writing poetry.

I thank my family for the love and support they have given me throughout my life.

My profound acknowledgment to the people of my tribe for raising me, as it takes a community to raise a person.

I express my gratitude to Elizabeth A. Garcia-Janis for organizing, collaborating and editing this book with me.

Contents

III. Love

IV. Hope

OUR LAKOTA LIFE

Tipi Nature

Our ancestors
did not have windows

For one thing
it was just unnecessary work
senseless
no common sense

Because all you had to do
is just step out
outside
and just look

But actually see
and be a part of nature

Natural way of life
be a part of nature
Being nature
Living nature

You wonder looking back

Where and when
did white people
become so unnatural

And now
WE
are becoming unnatural

We're not destroying
Grandmother Earth, per say
What we're doing
in our unnatural way

Is destroying Grandmother Earth's
natural resources
for us
to sustain life

In our unnatural way
we are destroying
the balance of life

on this Grandmother Earth

Our mother

for her to keep us alive
She feels so sad about that
She's trying so hard
to correct us
her children

But we won't listen

We keep doing unnatural stuff
we keep misbehaving

We won't listen

Grandmother Earth
Our mother feels sorry for us
She feels sad
And she's crying

She's losing her children
Through sickness
sicknesses

Many sicknesses

She'll be alone soon
She'll be lonely

she'll miss us

You see,
she's not dying
We are

She'll live on
And she knows this
She can see the future
She sees us

She's trying to show us
She's trying to tell us

But we won't listen

Our ancestors
did not have windows
in their tipis

Their tipi
was not a house
it was nature
it was part of
Grandmother Earth

Our ancestors did not
have windows
it made no sense

We did not have to look out
we were already out there
we were nature
natural

We lived
with our mother

and now
WE DON'T

Industrial revolution started
when the wasichu
stepped on turtle island
HERE

She's TRYING TO
TELL US

But we won't listen
And she's crying. *

I Was Asked

I was asked
Are you gonna take over
that tiospaye?

Is there anyone
That can take you
You can beat
anyone of those guys

I said,
I will not do that
I will respect that family

And go by their rules
I am a guest there
Treated kindly and respectfully

Treated with honor
I will treat them
with honor

There will be
no bullying
to them
by me
to take over

Why would you ask that?
Do you do that?

Young men
marry into a tiospaye
and take over

Is there anyone
who can take you?

I
I am that man
of my tiospaye
that will stand
I can take him

That bully
who married into
my tiospaye

I am the leader
of my tiospaye

Fair. Honest. Honorable.

I will treat him
kindly and respectfully

Will treat well
when treated well

If he is a bully
I
I am that man
that will stand

For my tiospaye
I can take him

Why do you ask that?

Hechitu yelo*

A Break-Up
Alcohol

Doesn't just want you
occasionally
on holidays
social occasions
on weekends
on evenings
in the afternoon

Alcohol wants you
Alcohol wants you

every hour
every minute
every second

to think of only...

to be your
go to

when it gets tough

when you get tired
when you feel down

to be your friend
alcohol
wants to be
your best friend

alcohol
wants to be
your only friend
your everything

when you quit
take a break
break-up

you feel like you lost
oh such a loss
your best friend

and when it gets too hard
you go back to it
alcohol
and ohhh...
it feels so good
at first

then it begins again
the disagreements
the arguments
the put-downs
the self-pity
the anger
the lashing out
the blaming

and then
need to take
a break again

and it happens
over and over
a vicious cycle

of a deep and meaningful
and very
very
emotional and loving
relationship

It's hard to see
the damage
and yet

you do
But you deny
Love is blind

And when it's time
to truly
break-up

It is hard

The loss
of my best friend
my love
for
alcohol

Mni wakan*

Promise Us No more

Promise us no more
white man
give us no more grief

The Black Hills
are really ours
that is a fact
Not just belief!

Promise us no more
white man
we have no room
for you

Our hearts are filled
with pain
from all you put us through

I closed my eyes
and seen myself
shot in the back, by a friend

I closed my eyes
and seen my people
shot down
from the cavalry guns

Promise us no more
white man
we bow to you
no more

We have seen
Wakan Tanka
who opens up our doors

We will fight!
We will kill!
We will die!

Promise us no more*

My thoughts on "Promise Us No More"

I wrote this poem in 1976
a little while after
I got out of the army.
And I decided that it
wasn't the Indian people's
fault.

That we we are
fighting
one another.
It wasn't our fault

That we were living
in anger.
That confusion
was guiding us
and alcohol
was controlling us.

I wrote this poem
about the promise
the white man gave -
"...til the grass grows
and the waters flow..".

I was angry then
and ready at that time
to fight if need be
to kill
or die,
whatever.

For a cause
called survival.
To be a warrior
To right the wrong
done to
our people

And I look back now
I was not so wrong
Even though
I was drinking

But I was drinking
and the alcohol
is confusing us.

The alcohol and the drugs
are controlling us.

And a man, the other day
said that he has
seen people
control their lives
while they still drank.

All I have seen
when people drank -
was that they were
out of control.

Because a dark spirit
was hanging over them.
I see that now.

We are at a time to forgive
ourselves
and the people around us

In order to live
a happy life
a good and decent life.

Because we don't have
to beat our wives
to be a man

We don't have
to gang other men
to feel strong

nor abuse our children
to feel power

All we have to do is -
not take
alcohol or take drugs.

That is the challenge
for our men today.*

The Fever

The fever
They got the fever
They got the fever
And took our very lives

Were they bad people
We ask

What are they?
Some power
greater than
themselves.

Meaning that they
themselves
did not think
it wrong
That they had
a right to do
what they did.

Manifest destiny
as defined

The belief or doctrine
held chiefly in the
middle

And latter part of
the 19th century
That it is the destiny
of the U.S.
to expand its territory
over the whole of
North America
and to extend
and enhance
its political,
social,
and economic
influences

The destiny of the U.S?

What right did they have
to decide this destiny?
at our expense

To destroy
a race of people
as a whole.

They got the fever
the fever
to destroy
and take.

To take
as it pleases them.

We as the survivors.
We as the defeated?

We are not defeated!!
We survived their
destiny
But what a cost!
What a human
and natural cost.

They, now, fulfilling
their destiny,
are destroying
all life.

To extend and enhance?
They got the fever –
and took
our very lives. *

United

There is no real
USA
It was always a myth
A fantasy

An idealist country
with idealistic people
never realist

United?

Really?

It was always
based on
murder and lies

And theft
And greed
And more
materialistic

Never fairness

Never equal race

United
States
Really?

This is the human race
of the USA

And today
it showed
its true colors

Today
Yesterday

2016 to 2020

Tomorrow?

United?

Now. Sadly
it will continue to
deteriorate
and self destruct

Unless

And there is always
An unless

Unless

To change
To unite

Which was never
really done

Maybe
for a moment

World Wars I and II

Maybe?

But was it
For a moment

Really?

Segregation
United
Really?

Fight for me
in your lesser place

A moment?
United?
really?

Idealistic
never realistic

Can we?
Really?
Unless

There is always
an unless
Unless

To change
To unite
To love
One another

To be
or to die

Mother Earth is watching.*

Heroes of Our People

You hear the stories
of these heroes of our people
The deeds they did
the glory
the fight to the finish.

These heroes of our people
The war for our land
The battles there were many.

The war of one
is in there
The war of two
is in there
Of the world
one and two.

The heroes of our people
the wars for our land
Korea
is in there
Vietnam
is in there
of the conflicts of the war.

Our people are still strong.

It was like that then
to save the world
to save the whole world
These heroes of our people.*

Pushed Down and Stepped On

We are here, we survived
We got his far
Our parents got us here
Their parents got them here
We got this far.

We were pushed down and stepped on
When once we were free.

They put us on this place
called that agency.

They fenced us in
We had to ask to move

And to push us down
and step on us harder

They didn't let us hunt for food.
And if we did...we were labeled
hostile
and hunted down.

And to push us down
and step on us harder.

They gave us rations
as they saw fit
If we didn't do as they said
they cut our rations
and we were starved.

To push us down
And step on us harder.

They gave us a plow, a few tools
a horse and a cow
And told us to live like them

To push us down
and step on us harder.

After we started to adapt,
and try to live with a plow and a cow
they changed the rules.

To push us down
and step on us harder.

They started to act
to take more land.

The allotment was a tricky plan.
They took more land.

To push us down
and step on us harder.

They took our children away from us.
They put them in boarding schools.

They took our language
And split our families.
They took our pride.

To push down
and step on us harder.

They put an outlaw on our religion
We prayed in secret
They took our spirit.

To push down
and step on us harder.

They gave us alcohol
firewater
to destroy each other.

We forgave
and we forgot
And we fought
and died for them,
when the great wars came.

To push down
and step on us harder.

They had to humor us.
They gave the anthros a study plan
to come with the ...New Deal.

To push down
and step on us harder.

They put another act
The anthros came up...with the IRA
and the government took out the I...
so we couldn't see.

We re-organized, we acted good
We plowed and we hayed.

We lost our pride and we got it back
They broke our spirit
We became more spiritual.

We are here...we survived.
We got this far.

To push us down
and step on us harder.

TO LIVE AND BE HAPPY
WITHOUT DRUGS AND ALCOHOL.

THE BLACK HILLS
ARE NOT FOR SALE!!!

Editor's Note: This chapter's poems are meant to raise awareness about historical trauma felt by many people in the reservation. It is meant as a poetic dialogue with the past colonizers. This poem is also meant to express the significance of the sacred Black Hills not being for sale and the importance of respecting the treaties.

SPIRITUAL STRUGGLES

Wild And Untamed: The Pain Of The Cage

I feel wild and untamed
So much energy
flowing inside
I run
and I hide
And I run some more.

And yet, I get nowhere
The pain of the cage.

I look around
I look all around
And there's nobody there
I look and I reach
And I grab for what I can.

And yet, I come up empty
The pain of the cage
the cage inside
inside my heart.

The lesson...

the lesson to learn
the pain of the cage
the cage of one
the prison of self
the lesson
What is the lesson?

I paced up and down
back and forth
from wall to wall
the pain of the cage

I try to stretch
but could not extend
I take a breath
but not enough air

I holler as loud
as I could
with all my might
'til my hair
stands at its ends.

And yet there is
no sound
the pain of the cage

I strike at all
that is near
with all the power
I possess
the force of evil and good
I use it all
in my attack.

Yet nothing moves
the pain of the cage
to give in
to let go.

To reach
and expect nothing
to run but not to hide
to holler, but in song
to feel wild and untamed
the flow
of a direction.

To strike
not with force
not with anger
not with evil
not with hatred
not without
nor within

not to strike
but to hold
with good
with patience
with love.

The lesson, of the pain
of the cage,
the cage within.*

To Say Something

Not saying anything
Is like saying, "Go ahead".

The teacher didn't say
to the Youth,
"That's not right;
look at your heart."

The Spirit Man
setting a price
to find a direction
to find God.

The father
didn't stand his ground
and set rules
and boundaries.

What is Wolakota?
What is Kola?
What is Kili?
What is Essee?
What is Homie?
What is gangster?

Generations of apathy
with their anger
they ask,
"Why do I have
to carry this?"

"Why didn't they take care
of this before?"
This...this apathy.

Why do I have to
correct it?!
Why do I have to
speak out?!

I need help
Where is the father
Who says nothing?

Where is the teacher
who shows me
no heart?

Where is the spiritual man
looking for glory?

I'll just join a gang.

Or...or, please!

Show us the way
to life
in Spirit

Please...say something.*

A Moment

A moment
An encounter
A brief time
Of physical contact
A temporary fulfillment
of meaningless affection.

The need to be held
To be comforted.
To be told
of admiration
of body and beauty.

Physical
not enough,
The ego
not enough,
No love
not enough
Sexual
not enough.

The heart,

inside
outside,
not enough.

Looking
always looking.

For the special
for the love
for a moment
of heart
crying inside.
hiding,
evading,
searching,
committing...?*

Fear

It hurts to think
It hurts to feel
It hurts to see

We're scared –
We're scared of our shadows
We're scared of the mirror

So we only touch the surface
Let's get deep
The fear
Let's face the fear.

Were we molested?
Were we abused?
Were we scared?

Yes, we were.

Let's get deep.
Face that fear.
Look in the mirror
Look at ourselves.

We had no time.
We're running out

The race of our people
are being born dead
Fetal Alcohol Syndrome
is like death.

A child is born pure
A child looks at a beer can
he sees death.

A man or woman
drunk every day
They are walking dead -
just didn't lie down yet.

And now our children
are being born
FAS

Let's get deep
Let's look in the mirror

If we look at our people
That's us
That's our mirror
When a high percentage
of our children are born FAS
That's our mirror
So, let's deal with it!

We as Indian people
have the power
the will
the faith
We have a Great Spirit
Tunkasila
Our prayers
Our cultures as Indian people.
We know how to solve FAS.

No white person
getting up here with
suit and tie
no matter how nice
no matter how polite
can tell us how to deal with
FAS

They are not us.
They did not grow up
all their lives
being Indians.

They didn't grow up
on reservations
and live the life.

Fear
Don't be scared
of the educated

Nice intellectual words
are not going to solve
the problem.
Spirituality
is going to solve
this problem
God and us.

Who are we?
And are we really seeing?

Are we scared
of our shadows?
Are we scared to look
in the mirror

Let's get deep.*

The Right To Be Respected

A very concerned woman
Didn't want to leave her name
She said she felt
the words;
she says
might help someone.

She lives here
on the reservation
born and raised here.

there are a lot of abuses
going on today, but
our children are
just being quiet about it.

Our children have a right to say
"This is not right."
And some are voicing
their right to be respected.

I am finding out some things
that are very hard to accept
or realize
Things that happened
with our people
in the past.

I am finding out that
there were abuses
that were hidden
kept quiet

Sexual abuses,
physical abuses.

I am finding out that
we as adults, some not all,
are trying to continue, the hidden,
or keep quiet
the physical and sexual abuses.

And our children are saying
"I have a right to be respected."
And it's true.
They do have that right.

Right now, we have to stop
the abuses that are happening
We have to forgive
our parents
for abusing us, or letting us
be abused.

We have to forgive
not only our parents
but ourselves.

We have to forgive
ourselves
And live a good life.
So our children
can live a good life.

And when we are grandparents
our grandchildren
will respect us.

We have the opportunity
today
to stop the cycle.
The vicious cycle of abuse
of mismanagement of our lives.

One of our men said
"We got knocked down to our knees".

This is true...

This is true...

We are abusing our children
We are abusing our elders
We are abusing our wives

Our 14 and 15 year olds
are getting pregnant

Let's look at ourselves
What are we doing?
What kind of an example
are we portraying?

Our children
are the mirrors
You look in a mirror
You see a reflection of
yourself.

You look at your children
they will reflect back
what you taught them
through example.

Let's stop it now!

We have to be honest with
ourselves
And take responsibility
for what's happening
in our home.

Let's do it now, my friends.
let's help our children
to be happy.

We can do this!*

This Warrior

This elderly we knew
Who walked on this earth
This man, as days go by
He knew, in a way, he knew.

Because of his way
His way of living
In his own way, he knew.

An old warrior knows these things.

These boys, these young men
They watched him

To figure his moves
When he had food
When he had money
When he was alone.

These young men, these boys
they watched him

They watched
When to steal
To take
To beat
from this old man
The life
The livelihood.

Of the way this man lived.

But this man
This old warrior
he knew, in a way he knew.

And they came
These boys, these young men
They came.

But they didn't just take
They destroyed a way of life
To be a man.

And now, they're sorry
They destroyed
themselves.

This warrior, he knew
In a way, he knew.

And with his death
This elderly abuse
That came to death.

These, are not men.*

Only A Moment

Felt the moment
And didn't let it pass!

Start feeling low, way low
How long will this last?
Only a moment
If you just let it pass.

Felt like hell on earth
feeling lost and alone
Couldn't muster up
that beautiful smile
Where had happiness gone?

In that moment
Of tears and self-doubt
She didn't want to live
She put that thing around her neck
She had her life to give.

She checked?!

In her mind, she said "Wait".
She changed her mind

She changed her mind
But it was too late.

In that moment...
of tears and self-doubt
She should've let it pass.

How long will this last?

She coulda reached out
She coulda called for help
Her friends woulda been
right there
Her family woulda been
right there
Her brothers,
her sisters,
her baby
The loves
all right there

She didn't have to do this thing

No one should go out this way
She didn't have to go

We asked why?
Only God knows
In that moment
Only God knows.
Why she had...to go.

She couldn't muster up
that beautiful smile
Where had happiness gone
For that moment
feeling lost and alone

How long is this gonna last?

Only a moment
if you just let it pass.

We all get that feeling sometimes
We feel all alone sometimes

How long will it last?
Only a moment
If we just...let it pass.*

No One Answered

She cried for help
She screamed for help
But no one answered.

We stand back
and we listen
But we make no move

We can grab her
and pull her out
But we make her scream
some more

By doing nothing.

We add to the pain

They're crying, you know
Our women
Our Lakota women.

With their strength
and their power
They're crying for help

No...
screaming for help.

They stand strong and look like
nothing's wrong.
The pride of the Lakota
And yet at night
when it's dark
her man beats her again.

And makes her do
the things she must

In the day
she shows no fear
"I can toe to toe with him.
I better not
My other eye will be
blackened too."

She's strong
Our Lakota women
But only on the surface

Her children know.

She cried for help.

She screamed for help
but no one answered.

She's screaming all the time
Even when she shows
no fear.

Where are our men today?
To protect our women
and children
Where are our warriors?

They're beating
our Lakota women.

"I'm due for another beating," she says.

Do our warriors
protect or terrorize
our women and children

What is a man?
Alcohol and drugs
do not make a man.

"I'll beat her. I'll be strong".

She is not the enemy
The Lakota women.

Her children know.

She cried for help.
She screamed for help.
But no one answered.

She is crying now.*

Powerless

To think of the dust I made
At the speed of my car
Driving across the dirt road
Tipping the beer
Everyone stand clear
I got the beer power.

The power
to be disillusioned
The power
to act tough
The power
to wreck
the beer power.

I ran into a horse
wiped it out
The beer power.

I ran into a deer
beer power.

I hit the ditch

Wiped out a fence
I flew over the approach
And rolled
My friend flew out
I found him dead
The power.
Beer power.*

The Silence

He opens the door
And slowly walks
into the dark bedroom.

She is sleeping quietly
And dreams of flowers, singing birds
and trees.

He kneels down beside her
her arms at first
to feel the softness

With heart beating fast
he pulls the covers down.

She wakes
with eyes big with fear
But cannot move
Looking at the wall

She closes her eyes
As if sleeping
Trying to shut out

What is about to happen.

With tears in her eyes
she silently cries.

And her heart
that is broken in two.

He does what he does
with force
and distorted love
and physical sex for two.

She whimpers
from the pain
But he says, "It's okay".

Her little heart broken
With nowhere to go
Nowhere to run.

In the hell
with no way out.

In the silence...
The silence.

And the silent scream
crying out.

My daddy...
"He hurt me".

"Please somebody
help me."
To find
the dreams
of flowers, birds and trees.

And return to innocence. *

Editor's Note: This poem and other poems written in this book
were written by the poet with empathy and compassion for those
who suffered physical and sexual abuse. In his work as a counselor,
he learned of the sufferings of his people even more. And he knew
that he had to air out what has caused suffering and raise more
awareness among the people in the Pine Ridge reservation so
those affected can get help.

The Light in Us

Love is God
God is love
the light is in us
God's spirit.

Darkness
is not us.
We are from God.
From the light.

Nothing
can come to us
around us
No darkness
No dark spirit
unless invited.

We did not invite this...
dark spirit
and demand that it leave.

Leave our children alone

Leave our elders alone
Leave our women alone
Leave our men alone
Leave our people alone.

We ask God
Take this dark spirit away
take it somewhere
where it won't hurt anyone.

We did not invite it.

God is love.

We love our children.
We love our people.
We love God.

God is love.

United we pray.*

Control

Feelings of emotions and stress
Control is very hard
We have so much to look forward to
In our own backyard.

You see
the man
You see
the woman
They're trying to
understand each other.

They sometimes use
the example
of their father and mother

I've seen my woman
talking to a man
I've seen my man
acting so strange.

My friends make fun
they are so mean

I beat one up
My woman
she just can't see.

She is laughing and talking
to another man there

She knows I am sad.

But doesn't she care?

Control
I have no control.

My man, he seems so mean
I'll laugh
and make him laugh
I'll just push it aside
My foolish pride
He'll be happy
on my behalf.

Feelings of stress
they got the best
the man
he lost control
and the woman
she didn't know.

You see
the man beat his wife.
he was drunk
and lost control.

He beat her so bad
is she dead
He is sitting there crying.
he doesn't know. *

Editor's note: This was another poem written to create awareness about spousal abuse. The poet hopes to encourage people to seek help.

I Know Him Still

A friend of mine died
He died some years ago
But I know him still
I remember him well.

One time, he grabbed me
from behind
And just threw me down.
I hit my head on the ground.
But I fought back.

I didn't give up.
he didn't give up.

We fought and wrestled
until we were tired.
And then we quit.

He said, "You have to be
ready to fight any time.
Even your friends sometimes."

I had a black eye
and a cut lip
He had a bloody nose.
We were best friends.

I know him still.*

Are You Strong Enough?

Are you strong enough
to face your fears?
To stand like a man
Against the problems
and struggles of today
without alcohol and drugs

Are you strong enough
to face your fears?
To be patient with your wife
and children
With words of encouragement
and love
Without alcohol and drugs

Are you strong enough
to face your fears
because we don't have to
beat our wives
to be a man...

We don't have to gang

other men to feel strong...
Nor abuse our children ...
to
feel power.

All we have to do
to not take alcohol
or take drugs
This is the challenge of our men
today

Are you strong enough
to face your fears?*

Do You Remember?

Do you remember
the time
you were nothing?

How could you?
You were nothing.

Then you were born.
You are...something.

But are you
really something?

Remember the time we were all
nothing?

But now.
Now...look.
We're all something.
Not just you.
Not just me.

We

are something
Not above, not below
but something.

Think...
then go on.*

Stand Up and Be free

When you fall into alcohol
You cannot climb out
When you are living with it
You are not living at all.

When you say it doesn't hurt
and you're doing nothing wrong
You're wrong.

When you blame someone else
You're living a lie.

Don't just sit back and say
I'll get by.

When you're letting alcohol
ruin your life
Don't lose your children
And don't lose your wife.

Because it hurts you
really bad
it cuts like a knife.

C'mon Lakota man!
You know you can.

Stand up
and be strong
Stand up
and be free

Because you know
who I'm talking about
I'm talking about
You
and me.*

Trees

I try to talk to the beaver
The trees are too young
How will they survive
He would not listen

The tree
is the center
of the great circle.

The beaver
does not care
he, too
must survive.

I try to talk to the trees
You must grow faster
The trees said
they cannot.

I told the trees
I'm sorry
I need heat
I, too
must survive

The tree said
"Fear not, human".
Life is short

All life will live
As we live, we learn.
As all animals.

For when the tree's life
is ended
So will all life end.*

Keep It Warm For You

I walked in the kitchen door.

We rented an old trailer
With an addition of a living room
With a wood stove
to heat the whole house.

It was nice and warm
when I walked in.
She was standing by the stove
in the kitchen
So pretty
I loved her.

It was about 6 in the evening
She was cooking
the kids playing
watching tv
I gave her a hug
and a kiss
and told her
my friend's car
gave out down the road

The carburetor gave.
I'm gonna go help him out
It won't take long.

She gave me
a warm smile
so loving
She asked, "You wanna eat first?"
I said, "No, I'll be right back."
She said, "Okay, I'll keep it
warm for you."

And that good feeling was there.
The warm and trusting feeling.
She gave me that look
when I helped other people
I said, "Okay."

I walked out the door
And drove away as planned

My friend was in the car
He said. "How did it go ?"
I said," She believed me."
And grabbed the beer

and drank it fast.

I came back two days later.
All alone.
It was snowing a little.
the house was empty and cold.
I was hanging over.
And wanted someone to hold me.

I looked over at the kitchen stove.
And couldn't think for a while.

I could remember a smile
And the soft and beautiful words
"I'll keep it warm for you."

And I hit the wall with my fist
And I cried. *

If She Were Mine

I saw a child
Hold back her tears
I left her alone
with all her fears.

I remember
when she was only four
She cried
So I went to her bedroom door.

I said, "What's wrong?"
But she wouldn't say
She just replied,
"Where's mommy?"
in her helpless way.

I held her tight
And I said, "Don't cry.
You're mother is gone but
she'll be back."
I'll stay right here
by your side.

And she looked at me
and cried.

It was only a year or two ago
it seems so long to me.
When this little girl
let me be her dad
and gave her love so free.

But the time came
when I had to leave
And the little girl
I had to leave behind.

I told her mother,
"she is so sweet, so innocent."
I love her
and wish she were mine.

As I was leaving
I said to this little girl
To be kind
and watch your mom.

She looked at me
in her helpless way
as if saying

please come back someday.

I saw a child
hold back her tears.

I left her alone
with all her fears.*

Desperate

I struggled with a log
trying to pull it uphill
the snow is knee-deep
I chopped up
two dead trees
by the creek.

I made them the size
a man could carry
or drag.

This blizzard
caught me by surprise.
It was close to spring
and warming up.
So I wasn't worried too much
about wood.

Then, all of a sudden
it started snowing
I had enough wood the first day...
plenty
that night

the wind picked up
and the next day
was an all out blizzard.

I looked out the window,
Damn!
What a day!
My wife didn't want to get out
of bed
She stayed in bed with baby
My 8 year old
didn't even peek her head
out of the covers
of her bed.

I got up and started the stove
in the living room.
Cry...it must be below zero
in the house.
I got the fire going
pretty good,
and put on my parka
(army surplus)

The best thing
they ever did for us poor Indians

was let us have
the U.S Armed Forces
left-over clothes.

I had to go out and get some more wood.
I went outside.
And I thought
it was cold in the house.

I had to re-adjust
my breathing
caught my breath twice
just to struggle for air.

The wind was blowing
and it was cold.

I went to the back of the house
in the direction of the creek
I couldn't see the tree-line
of the creek.

Across the creek was my sister's house
But I couldn't make that out either.

I went out and gathered
a couple of arm loads of wood.
Our wood supply
was pretty low;
and too many drifts
to get wood in a vehicle.
The only way
was by foot.

The house was warming up
a little.
But I had to get the fire
going good
And keep it going
Just to stay warm.

And our wood
wouldn't last out
a day.

So, now
here I am.

Struggling with a log
pulling it up
a drifted hill
in below zero weather.

Talk about rough and tough.
That's me.
Or am I just desperate?

Just desperate, I think.
Damn!
I should have gotten
more wood
when it was warmer. *

Nobody Loves A Poet

Nobody loves a poet
because you are not being
the way they want
yet they understand
what you write.

They feel your words
But cannot accept you
as yourself
They don't want you
in their world.
Because they cannot
control you.

The worth of power
is in the strength
of the heart.

And at your weak moment
they kick you
while you're down.

Maybe, that's to help you
get stronger

or maybe, it's to keep you there.

But your strength
is in your heart.
And you get stronger anyway.

And I thank the people
who are kicking me now.*

Darkness Fell Over the People

Darkness fell over the people
the sun was covered by clouds
the people couldn't see the light
the rainbow shines no more.

They're young, you know
these people
who seek the end
The full circle
to seek it fast.

Listen to the signs
Show you are for real
Explain that life is good
Stay close
You are a friend.

Darkness falls anytime
But light is inside
Seek the light.

These people who seek the end
the full circle
to seek it fast.

The end of hardship
of challenge
of growth

There is no end to these
But there is support of
friends.

Seek support of friends
and love
for health and life.*

It's Time

Almost like it's time
You had all this time
The last few hundred years
You had your fun.

You could have Done it right
You could have Made it good
The goodness was in your grasp
You had your run.

Mistakes have been made yet.
We look back and see the gains.
At times, you've done well
The wars, the deaths, the pain.

But at those times, You schemed
You lied to each other
You would kill your own mother
It seems, for land for money
For gain.

You killed us.
You raped us.

You took our food
You took our livelihood

You took our land
You shook our hand

And lied

You. Were not good.
You. Were not fair.
You. Were not clean.
You. Were dirty and mean.

Your scheme

Are you still today?
Yes.
The answer is yes.
You are still today

It seems

Almost like it's time
You had all this time
the last few hundred years

And all you did,
in your greed
In your time of grabbing
is left us all in tears.

Mother Earth is dying
Mother Earth is crying

Mother Earth
Oh, Mother Earth
Our Mother Earth
Our Mother

Through your greed and hatred
Through your time of taking
Through your destruction
Mother Earth is who you're
breaking

For us she grieves
She cries
She's sad
For us

You took our food
You took our livelihood
And Mother Earth
You took hers too.

You.
Are still taking today
Enough is never enough
You said you had it rough.

Almost like it's time
You. Me. We.
have to work together
in this stormy weather

Mother
Our Mother
Our Grandmother

Will not wait for us

You had your chance
We had our chance

Our livelihood
You took her too.

The rugged cross
is our cross too

It's almost...
Time's up.*

LOVE

Miracles

Not sure why
You touched my heart
Now my life is better
Miracles happened that day.

God made this happen
believe in angels
in grandfathers
Tunkasila's love
Our love will guide the way.

We never met
And yet Love met
Our love was there.

Before sight
in the past
in the future
now
in this moment
right here
Miracles happened that day.

before our eyes
I loved you
to love
before sight.

You loved me too
the love
for one person
to another
there's the light.

What becomes of us?
Love will decide
Trust
Miracles happened that day!

In our beautiful love
for each other
and life
the door is now open
Love
will guide the way.

And yes...
MIRACLES HAPPENED THAT DAY! *

We Follow His Candle

We're being guided from the beginning
God won't give us anything
we cannot handle.

We are directed
We're walking His walk
We follow His candle.

We can change our minds
We're free
We have decision-making
ability.

But if we let Him guide us
We won't go wrong
It's His mission
that we do.

Yes, we're human
and we have all these emotions
God knows these too.

But He won't give us anything
we cannot handle
We're walking His walk
We follow His candle.

I love you, Liz.
Your heart
Your body
Your mind
Everything about you
spiritually.
Your love
You are so kind.

In this time in our lives
Let's enjoy today.
I love you now and forever
Let's let the past lay.

You and I together
we can do anything.
We can dance,
we can draw
play music
sing
do anything.

God won't give us anything
we cannot handle.
We're walking His walk
We follow His candle.*

With Eyes Wide Open

With eyes wide open
And hearts filled with joy
For a new adventure.

Our life guided by God
Who gifted our love
And planned our future.

We are
because we love
one another.
And together
from the beginning
we knew
God did this.

We're guided and protected
and loved
by God
from God
with God
in His light

We're in this.

For all our life
with you, my wife
with eyes wide open
God beyond
more than we know
love.

With eyes wide open
And hearts filled with love
and guided and protected
and yes,
and always,
from God above.

With you, my love
my heart,
my life
forever and more
My love
of my life
my beautiful wife.

In this I know
eyes wide open
together

you and I

for a new adventure
of joy
For the rest of our life.

Love you, baby.*

You Are New

My love
my beautiful Elizabeth
You are new
to me
You are always my new.

Thank you
we will enjoy our new truck
I too am so excited
for us.

My darling
to marry you
a gift from God
our love.

WE will have the best time ever
All of us
family and friends.

We're as a flower
in bloom

We are as one.
One heart.
We are soooo close...
so one.
they can't tell us apart.

I am You
And you are me.
In this way
through God
we are free.

Love you
so much
with all my being
with you
I am able
I am seeing.

I've always loved you
before time began
I loved you
Life and time
are little
compared to my love
for you

In my life
I never truly
loved anyone
but you.

Only God
had my heart
before you
in this life.

But truly
I've always loved you
before time began.

And now...
And forever
I love you. *

No Matter

Of all the places
people and things
for me
You are who
I want to be with

No matter where we are
No matter what we do
No matter the things we have
I am loving life with you.

My happiness
my walk in life
my love for all my life
is you
my wife.

My wife
Ohhh...
how I love the sound
my wife
for life
of life.

To walk in God's light
You and I.*

My Medicine Bag

Thank you, my love
For finding
my medicine bag
with my rock in it.

Thank you, my love
for being my wife
Filled full of love
You openly give it.

I think of you
all the time
I miss you
when you're not there.

I pray
for your safe-keeping
That God
protects us everywhere.

I love you
with all my heart

your smile

your laughter.

The way you hold my hand
the way you wake up
and say,
"Are you okay?"

The way you walk down the street
and laugh
and talk
I love your way
our way.

My beautiful wife
my life. *

Love from the Start

I love you, baby, with all my heart
We both felt that love from the start.

Words cannot express this loving feeling
so deep
It's amazing to me surrounded by God's light
Safe in His keep.

I think of you, every second
Every minute, every hour
of every day.
You're in me, you're around me
We're one, in every way.

I am the greatest, luckiest of men
On this earth
Wrapped in your love, spiritual from God
feeling like rebirth.

And so I say this
Wopila tanka
Tunkasila.*

To Love

You're my coconut tree
You're my love
of my life
You're my life
of my love.
With you
I'm free.

To love
beyond belief
My dream woman
My sunshine
My air
My calmness
My stress-relief
You're my everything.

Now and forever
and ever.*

A New Year

Happy New Year
My love of my life
Thank you for being you
and loving me so much
through all my faults.

I will continue to love you
And protect you
And take care of you.

I will always be your friend
Stay healthy
and happy
for both of us.

Continue to exercise
meditate
and pray daily.

I will be there for you.
And willing to help you
any way I can.
As long as you want

to keep working.

I will comfort you
And protect
and make love
to you.

In our beautiful life
provided
by God.

For us together
I'll always be grateful and thankful
For God
bringing us
together. *

Love is

Love is, we are
This is better
We, you and I
We are love.
God made this gift.
You are the gift
of love
to me.

God made it so
Yes, within our love
is more,
We, through God.

Love in love.

Can it get better?

Yes.

All is possible
in love.

Better times ahead
Ohhh...
we are so blessed.

Better times ahead
God makes it so...
wonderful.*

My Everything

A flower
blooms in the spring
the birds sing

Every beat of my heart
for you
You are
my everything.

My Only

My beautiful
my lovely
my wonderful
my one and only.

You are the one
for me
the only
my only
I have no other.
I am not lonely.

For anyone but you
My mind
thinks only of you.

I absorb you
in me
my thoughts
my mind
my heart
my spirit.

I and you
are one.*

Colors

The moon is like the sunset
And sunrise in one
the full moon, that is
full of love
full of light
and colors
All colors.

Our love
all different colors
of emotions
new
powerful
exotic
filling
exciting
and yet, calming.

Full of light
from God.
Walk in His light.

Oh how amazing
you are.

You are a gift
to me.
We
are each other's
gift.

The sunrise, the sunset
the full moon.

The colors
of our love
our gifts from God.*

I Miss You Not

I miss
you...
not

I love and
am
I AM
with you.

I don't miss you.
Because
you are in me
you are me
daily
hourly
minutely

Every second
you're
with me.

I am so, so
glad I don't
miss you.
Our love
is pure
is real
is everything.

In the morning
at noon
at night
all day
our love.

I don't
miss you.
I'm with you.
Love
is God
WE
ARE
IN
LOVE.*

Love Is In the Air

Love our weekend together
We are a loving and hugging couple
Our life together
Like a bright sunshiny weather.

I love you so much
And delighted in our happiness
We have so much to look forward to
We are so blessed.

Love is in the air
Our hearts have met in there
Our love is sensitive
and need loving care.

I love you so
as well you know.

And you love me
delighted in our happiness.
To love and be free

Love each other.*

A Part of me

Oh how good I feel
Knowing you are a part of me
I have this warmth
I have this earthy feeling
to be free.

You have this way
to make me
love you.

You have this
This comfort too
with you.

I melt
in your arms
This earthy feeling
Home
is you
to me
to be free.

I have never...
never
never
ever
felt this good.

Hmmm
I could
I would
I should
I will
continue
to feel this good.

Life here
on earth
this life
ohhh how good life is
with you.
Ohhh how good it is.*

Gratitude

I have been
in a storm
of uncertainty
like a loss
of sense of direction.

I have felt lonely
and yes, alone.

I have gone
within myself
and no one
relative or friend
have I let in.

Through the years
I have managed
my content
of isolation.

And through it
At the time
happiness

sadness
loneliness
as one.

Love??
A hint
a glimpse
a dim glimmer
a hope
a possibility.

Love??
Only family
and God.

I had
no need
for another
I
was enough.

And then
Ooohhhh
and then...

And then...

I met you.
Ooohhhh
I met you...

Ooohhhh God
I met you.

A tear
of gratitude
to God.

I met you
and love.

A tear
of gratitude.

I MET LOVE.

True.
Real.

I can touch it.
I can feel it.
I can taste it.

I see,
again.
I breathe
it.

Love.

I am
We are.*

Journey

Loving you
is my journey
It's road glowing brightness
It's a life, I am.

This is our time
To shine
Our life light
It's ours
together.

Love makes it so.
And so
we glow.

God's love is us.

Spiritual light inside.
To see...
You and I
in God's light.

We walk
in prayer
in love
each other
One.

In my journey
It's road glowing brightness
It's life, I am.

This is our time to shine
Our life light
is ours
together.

Love makes it so
And we glow.

God's love is US
Spiritual light inside
To see...
you and I
in God's light.

We walk in prayer
in love

each other
One.*

HOPE

We Can Start Now

Are we adventurous people?
We have always been adventurous
there is much adventure out there
in this world right around us.
We're just missing it.

It seemed appropriate to say these words
because we are struggling
with ourselves.

When all we have to do
is live and be happy
yet we're fighting each other
and taking drugs and alcohol.

We don't know what nature is any more
We don't know what it feels like
to breathe normal.
We don't know what it feels like
to just drink water.

And not take drugs.
And not smoke joints
And not drink alcohol.

And we don't know what it feels like
to be normal.

But we could know
Our children could know
Their children could know.

We could start now.
We could show our wife a good life.
We could show our children
a good life.
We could show ourselves
a good life.

All we have to do is drink water
and breathe normal
and face our fears
without drugs, joints and
alcohol.*

We'll Survive

What do we say
we'll survive
No...let's say
we'll live.

Let's say
our children will live
Let's say
their children will live.

Let's not think
Let's believe.

Grandfather
you are with us.
We are with you.
We pray to live.

Not just survive
but to live.

The grass still grows

The wind still blows

The streams flow
And the trees
Yes...the trees.

When the trees die
All life dies.
The trees live.

The eagle that circles all
is still with us.

The spirit we hold inside
of ourselves
Circles with the eagle
we are one.

But we are human
We are afraid
Let's not just survive
Let's believe.

Let's face our fear

and live.

In the circle
of the eagle
and begin
again.*

Snowflake

The snowflake touched the surface
of a weathered face
leathered
by time.
Hardened
by past experience.

The snowflake
pure
to clean
pure
to cover
pure
to comfort.

The face
hardened with time
hardened with pain
hardened with frowns

The rough face of time

The snow-covered
comforted
smothered
froze
killed
took the pain... away.

The snowflake
pure
to clean
pure
to cover
pure
to comfort.*

I Climbed Up A Hill

I climbed up a hill
And couldn't climb down
Did I do it wrong?
Did I get on top?
The wrong way

I'm on top
But I'm all alone
And can't get down
Can someone come up?
Come and visit
It's dark
I'm afraid
If I walk, I'll fall.

Where am I?
I remembered climbing
Did I climb up?
or did I climb down?
And where's the light?
Who am I?
Let's see the light.

I climbed up a hill
And I couldn't climb down
After a time of despair
A time to look at myself.

With no light
And see...
and really see
And alone...
to be alone.

It's dark
And to see
And alone
You're full content
And there is a light
After a time
to really see.

Who am I?
The light is inside
I can see
the hill.
There is no hill.
I'm in a hole
and I can climb out.

to the real world...
and live.*

A Dream

One night I had a dream
In this dream
I somehow came to be
in this cave.
There I met an old man
who did not speak to me.

He just sat there over his fire.
I walked up to him.
He stood up and took my hand.

Soon, we were flying out of the big opening
of the cave
He didn't speak
We flew over trees
and hills
and creeks
and all living things.

I remember no more of the dream
My journey did not end
No conclusion.

I think about this dream.
Why did Grandfather not speak?
Why did he take me over my people's land?
Why did we not land,
my journey had no meaning?

Yet, it had great meaning.

My life is like this dream
I have not yet found my place
on this earth.
My spirit flies and searches
When I find my place
When I am fulfilled within myself
My Grandfather
will place me in my place.

I am now searching
I am now being open-minded
Mistakes are human
And they will not slow me down.

I will work in life
And find me
And wait for my dream again
to be placed in my place.*

Remember to Pray

Remember to pray
Pandemic is still here.
Be careful
Life is precious

They say short
Not so

Life is long
Let it be long
and happy
Good memories

Life
so beautiful
So much
has happened

Life is long
Live long
and be happy

Make every day
a good memory
avoid anger
when you can

And make sure
you can

Remember to pray
not for a god
or for a faith
but for Life

Your life
Your children's life
Your family's life
for all life

Because prayer is real
Prayer is spiritual
Prayer is physical
Prayer is emotional

Learn to pray
for you
You will feel
The lift

The lift
of weight
of energy
of self worth

Prayer can free you
and then
Life...will
Not be short

Life will be long
and happy

Prayer is life

Remember to pray.*

Afterword

I hope that you enjoyed my poems. I also hope that you got a glimpse and feeling of the Lakota life on the reservation as seen through my eyes.

I am happy to share my life with you. I am also looking forward to share more poetry with you in the near future. Liz and I are also in the process of writing a book entitled A Spiritual Warrior and His Lady Doctor.

Thank you for making the time to read my poetry book.

God bless you all.

Lawrence John Janis

Printed in the United States
By Bookmasters